AIRBORNE ANIMALS
How They Fly

Airborne

HOW THEY FLY

Animals

by GEORGE S. FICHTER

illustrated with photographs,
and with paintings
by JEAN ZALLINGER

GOLDEN PRESS
NEW YORK

CREDITS
Arthur Frock: 16; The National Audubon Society
—photographers—G. Ronald Austing: 43 (top and
bottom), 44; Allan D. Cruickshank: 41; Treat David-
son: 62; John H. Gerard: 54; Robert Hermes: 53;
L. L. Rue III: 40, 61; Hugh Spencer: 75

CONTENTS

The World's First Fliers

THE WORLD'S first flying animals were insects. Fossil remains show that they appeared on the earth about 300 million years ago. For more than 100 million years afterwards—until flying reptiles and birds developed—insects were the only winged creatures in existence.

Many of these ancient insects are known to scientists only by their wings, for their soft bodies were not easily preserved as fossils. The best specimens have been found embedded in amber, the fossilized resin of pine trees. Other insects left impressions in fine deposits of shale and limestone.

During the Coal Age, the period when insects developed rapidly, cockroaches were the dominant animals in the world. More than 500 kinds have been identified from their fossil remains. Many of them were

Present-day dragonflies resemble
their ancient ancestors, although no modern
day species is nearly as large as those we know
from their fossils (top).
Ancient dragonflies
that soared over swamps in the Coal Age
had wing spans of 30 inches (left).

7

large, although no larger than some of the giant cockroaches found in the tropics today. But cockroaches did have wings, used for short, fluttering flights. They still do today. They are the most ancient family of winged insects that still exist on the earth today.

Cockroaches were not the largest of the ancient winged insects, however. Enormous dragonflies, forerunners of present-day species, soared over the primeval swamps. Some of them had wingspreads of two-and-a-half feet!

Cockroaches of today are little different from those that lived 300 million years ago.

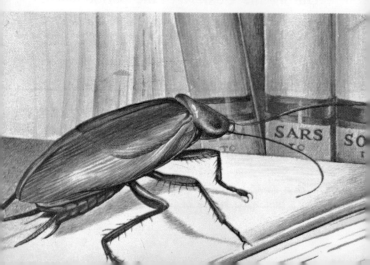

Insects: How Far and How Fast?

SOME years ago a French scientist made an amazing discovery: he found that bumblebees are too heavy to fly. This was certainly true according to his careful mathematical calculations. Men who knew about the French scientist's report watched the bumblebees fly by with new admiration, marveling at their ability to do what was impossible.

Since then, many other scientists have studied the flight of insects. They agree that, in general, insects are poorly designed "flying machines." Man-made aircraft are far more efficient. Yet insects were skilled at flying several hundred million years ago, and man has been flying not yet a century.

An insect's wings are completely different in structure from the wings of any other flying animal. They are neither developed from nor attached to any of the insect's three pairs of legs. Rather, they are direct outgrowths of its body wall. In most insect groups, wings do not appear until the insect

Life Cycle of a Butterfly

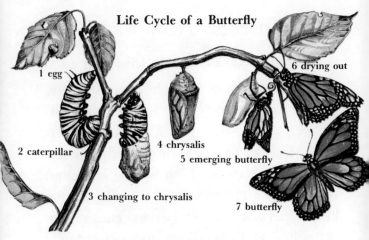

1 egg

2 caterpillar

3 changing to chrysalis

4 chrysalis

5 emerging butterfly

6 drying out

7 butterfly

**A butterfly's wings are limp and moist at first
but they soon dry and stiffen.**

reaches its adult stage. Then, as the insect
emerges from its pupa case, its wings begin
to unfold. At first they are wet, crumpled
pouches. Within a few minutes, however,
the insect's body fluids begin to drain out
of them. The membrane dries to tissue
thinness and is stretched tightly over the
hardened veins.

An insect's wings are kept in motion by
heavy, powerful muscles which are capable
of working for long periods of time without
tiring. The flight muscles that move a fly's

wings, for example, make up about one-fourth of the fly's total weight.

In flight, the common house fly may vibrate its wings more than 300 times per

An insect's wings are an outgrowth of its body wall and are moved by strong muscles.

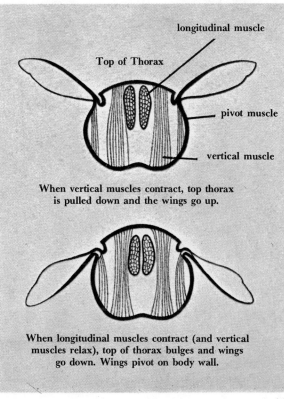

longitudinal muscle

Top of Thorax

pivot muscle

vertical muscle

When vertical muscles contract, top thorax is pulled down and the wings go up.

When longitudinal muscles contract (and vertical muscles relax), top of thorax bulges and wings go down. Wings pivot on body wall.

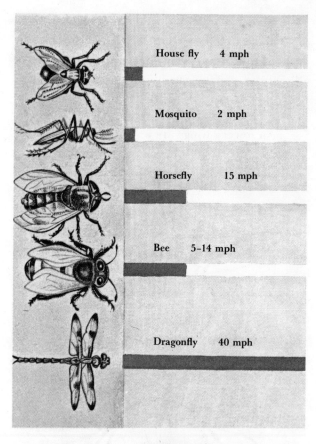

House fly	4 mph
Mosquito	2 mph
Horsefly	15 mph
Bee	5-14 mph
Dragonfly	40 mph

Few insects are capable of fast speeds
for extended periods of time.

second—as many as 20,000 times a minute.
Yet the fly's ordinary flight speed is only
about four miles per hour. A mosquito is

even slower—about two miles per hour. Horseflies can fly about 15 miles per hour, and botflies may be a bit faster. Hawk moths are also speedy, but dragonflies are the fastest. They can fly more than 40 miles per hour. Some midges can vibrate their wings more than 1000 times per second.

In proportion to its size, of course, even the house fly travels at an astonishing rate of speed. To match it, a big airplane would have to go several thousand miles per hour.

Interestingly, a dragonfly cannot fold its broad, straight wings when it rests. They are always stretched out. Also, both dragonflies and damselflies move their front and hind wings independently in flight. Thus, when the hind wings go down, the front wings go up—and vice versa. There is never a pause in their driving power in flight.

In contrast, the wings of most insects— and there are usually four wings, two on each side—are held together during flight. In bees and wasps this is accomplished by a row of hooks along the front edge of the hind wing. These hooks fit into a fold along the back edge of the front wing.

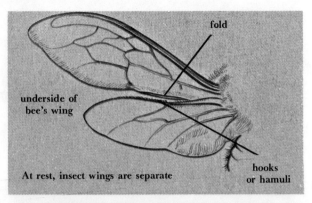

fold

underside of
bee's wing

hooks
or hamuli

At rest, insect wings are separate

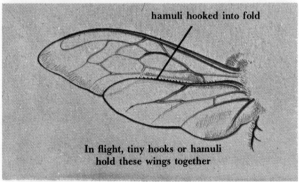

hamuli hooked into fold

In flight, tiny hooks or hamuli
hold these wings together

Front and hind wings of most insects are held
together by hooks so they move in unison.

Many moths and butterflies have lobes pro-
jecting from the rear edge of the front wings.
These slip into a fold of the hind wing. Such
devices lock the wings together so that they
work in unison.

Exactly how does an insect fly?

First, size and weight are in its favor, for these two factors determine the speed at which an object is pulled to earth by the force of gravity. A small, lightweight object naturally stays in the air more easily than a large, heavy one. A speck of dust, for example, can float in the air almost indefinitely. Likewise, there are insects so tiny that, because of their small size alone, they can remain in the air with no effort.

Also, a great many insects are made buoyant and balloon-like by pockets of air inside their bodies. Air reservoirs fill most of the honeybee's body cavity, for example.

Grasshoppers have air chambers inside their bodies which make them easily airborne.

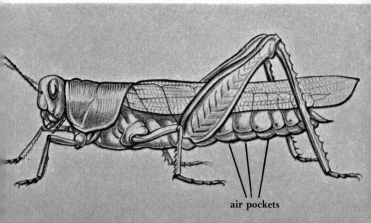

air pockets

Cicadas and grasshoppers have large air chambers inside their bodies. The entire digestive tract of the adult mayfly, which does not eat at all in its winged stage, is inflated with air so that these fragile creatures are easily airborne.

Once in the air, at any rate, many insects have little trouble staying there. Some, such as grasshoppers, jump off the ground. Others launch themselves from high places—the tips of blades of grass, the ends of branches, or the trunks of trees.

Thousands of mayflies cluster around strings of bright lights on warm summer evenings.

Some kinds make short flights. Others simply spread their wings and glide back to the ground. Most grasshoppers, for example, are poor fliers. As a rule, their flight is a long, slanting path carrying them back to the ground. But grasshoppers have been seen more than a thousand miles at sea, and aided by the wind, they often feed hundreds of miles from their hatching grounds. Truly sky-darkening clouds—as many as a hundred million 'hoppers in one seething, gyrating mass—will cover several hundred square miles as they move along. Mosquitoes have been observed more than a mile above the earth, and bees have been seen six miles above the earth.

Most butterflies keep themselves in the air with the simplest sort of insect flight. Some kinds flap their wings fewer than 10 times per second. They really "flutter" as they fly because they tend to lose altitude between the slow strokes of their wings. On the downstroke, the air beneath their wings is compressed, and in this same instant, the air pressure above their wings is lessened. So the air below pushes upward, providing the "lift" that keeps the butterfly in the air. These "up and down" strokes, however, give them almost no forward motion.

An insect does not simply flap its wings up and down when it flies, of course. The better it flies, in fact, the more complex are its wing movements. A good flier can pivot its wings so that air pushes from behind them as well as from beneath. This gives the insect its forward motion. It also rotates its wings so that they describe a "figure 8" pattern. The size of the loops in the figure 8 are varied with the wind and the direction the insect is traveling. In forward flight, the figure 8's are tipped to the rear, the wings moving forward on the downstroke. Insects that fly backward reverse the motion of their wings, tipping the figure 8's to the front, too.

In turning or flying sideways, an insect may slow down or even stop the vibration of its wings on one side. And some insects can also hover. They vibrate their wings rapidly up and down but do not move forward or backward or change their altitude. Good fliers have also mastered the art of

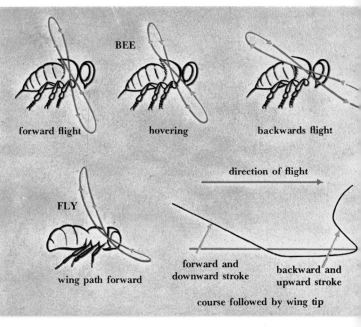

BEE

forward flight   hovering   backwards flight

direction of flight

FLY

wing path forward

forward and
downward stroke

backward and
upward stroke

course followed by wing tip

Tips of wings trace a figure 8 pattern in flight;
wings are pivoted to change direction.

flying into the wind to keep themselves airborne and on a level course.

Dragonflies are especially skilled at such
maneuvers. No other flying animals can
match their agility in the air.

We really know many insects best by the
whirr of their wings. Mosquitoes make a
whining, high-pitched note as they fly. The

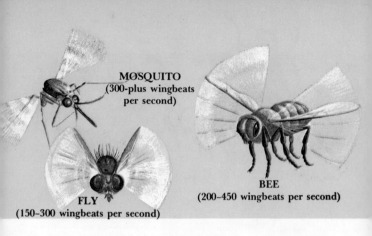

MOSQUITO
(300-plus wingbeats
per second)

BEE
(200-450 wingbeats per second)

FLY
(150-300 wingbeats per second)

low drone of botflies reminds us of sleepy spring afternoons. The buzz of a bee is ordinarily a busy sound, but we can also tell when the bee is angry or when it is tired by the pitch of the note made by its vibrating wings. June bugs are boisterously noisy in flight, and grasshoppers make "clicking" noises when they fly.

Some insects use their wings as noise-makers even when they are not in flight. Again, these are best developed among the grasshoppers and crickets. Some scrape the hind wings against the front wings, causing the front wings to vibrate. Others have special scrapers on their legs, and these are drawn over the wings to cause the vibration.

Most insects have two pairs of wings. Flies, however, are exceptions among the

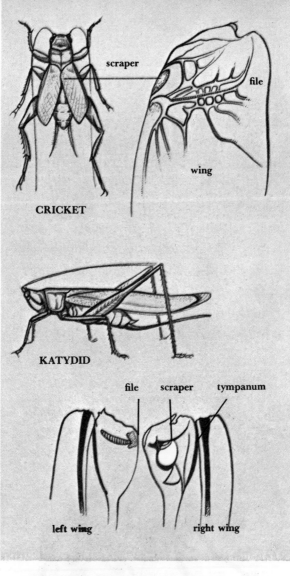

CRICKET

scraper

file

wing

KATYDID

file   scraper   tympanum

left wing   right wing

Mosquitoes, flies, and bees make droning
noises during flight. Crickets and katydids
have sound devices on their wings.

good fliers, for they have only one pair of wings. Their hind wings have been reduced to small knobs, called halters, which stick out on each side of their bodies. They assist in flight by serving as organs of balance. They are the fly's gyroscopes. As the fly takes off, these knobs fill with blood and then vibrate at the same speed as the fly's wings. When the fly lands, the halters deflate and become limp knobs.

One of the fly's most remarkable feats, a performance which puzzled scientists for a long time, is its ability to land upside down

The hind wings of a fly are reduced to knob-like structures (halters) that serve as organs of balance during flight.

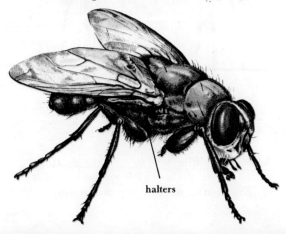

halters

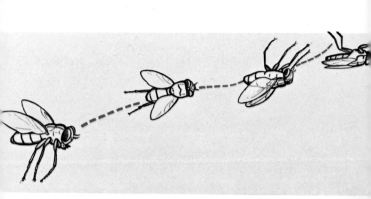

Slow-motion photography shows that flies
do a half-roll to land upright on a ceiling.

on a ceiling after flying along in a normal
feet-down position. The shift occurs more
quickly than the eye can follow. One early
explanation was that the fly did a loop-the-
loop, stopping on the upswing the instant
its feet touched the ceiling. Slow-motion photography finally provided the answer. The
fly actually does do a half-roll, turning upside down but with its head still pointed in
the original direction of flight.

Oddly enough, a fly's wings do auto-
matically stop vibrating the instant its feet
touch some solid object. This sort of convenient flight-stopping mechanism is not
unusual among insects. In some cases it is

23

associated with the presence or absence of light. Some moths, for example, can vibrate their wings only when it is dark. In the gradual change from night to day, this is not ordinarily a problem for them, but what happens when there is a quick change is interesting to observe. For example, if a moth is flying through a darkened room, it will drop helplessly to the floor when a light is switched on. Other insects react in the opposite way and can only operate their wings in the presence of light.

Fragile as they may seem to be, some insects do manage to make astonishingly long flights. Most unbelievable are the long

Wings of some insects stop vibrating when a light is turned on.

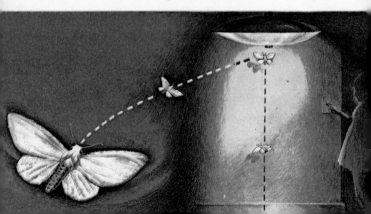

Flocks of monarch butterflies migrate from as far
north as Canada to the Gulf in winter.

migrations of certain butterflies. Monarchs
are the most famous. Each autumn they
begin southward flights, traveling from
Canada to the Gulf of Mexico. Along the
way they stop at night to rest in trees. Year
after year the same trees become clustered
with monarchs, and if the tree is cut down,
the next year's migration flight flutters over
the vacant spot for a long while before settling for another. In the spring, some of the

monarchs, their wings frayed and nearly scaleless, head northward to their old haunts.

Monarchs have even appeared in England, apparently having flown the Atlantic with the help of the wind. There are also butterflies that make migration flights from North Africa to northern Europe and others that cross the Mediterranean Sea. Painted Lady butterflies travel from New Zealand to Australia, a distance of some 1,000 miles over the ocean, and from California to Hawaii, about 2,000 miles.

Other insects, too, are seen flying over the ocean or other large bodies of water. Sometimes these voyagers are literally "at sea." They are victims of a strange natural phenomenon.

As the morning sun begins to warm them, some insects turn their bodies to get its direct rays. Others "race" their wings as they get ready for flight. Then the gentle morning wind begins to blow over the land from the water. The insects head into it on their take-off, just as other flying animals and airplanes do. And they continue to fly into the wind until eventually they come to land or the wind shifts—or, as often happens, they are exhausted. Then they fall into the water and become food for the fish.

Strangest of the insect fliers, perhaps, are the fairy flies, tiny wasps that can swim as well as fly. They lay their eggs on the young of insects found under the surface of the water in fresh-water streams and ponds. They swim using both their legs and wings. Out of the water their wings quickly dry and become organs of flight.

Fairy flies are small wasps that use their wings for swimming as well as for flying.

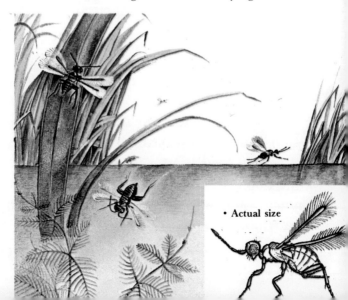

• Actual size

Flying Dragons

IT WAS 100 million years after insects got their wings before any other creatures took to the air. Then two groups of animals—reptiles and birds—developed wings at about the same time. Reptiles, dominated by the great and fearsome dinosaurs, were already the ruling creatures on land. Birds were newcomers to the world.

Flying reptiles, a specialized order of reptiles, were the strangest creatures ever to be airborne. Many different kinds developed during their years of existence. Some were no larger than sparrows. Others were weird giants—the largest animals that have ever flown through the sky. *Pteranodon,* the biggest of them all, had wings that spanned more than 25 feet. Yet its small, hollow-boned body weighed less than 25 pounds.

One group of these "flying dragons" had a slim and toothless birdlike beak. Sticking out behind their head was an equally long, knife-thin crest that apparently served as a rudder. Another group had short jaws which were studded with sharp teeth. Their tail, flat and spadelike, was probably used to steer them in their gliding flights. Others had large eyes. They probably hunted at night.

All of the ancient flying reptiles had similar wings, however. They were thin, leathery membranes of skin stretched between their front and hind legs. Most of the leading edge of the wing was supported by a greatly elongated little finger. The first three fingers remained free and were used as claws.

Their wings were variously shaped. Some were like huge sails; others were like curved scythes. But such wings were good only for gliding. A few of these airborne reptiles may have been able to fly by flapping their wings.

Pteranodon had a bony crest and 25-foot wing span. Its thin wing membranes stretched from a greatly elongated little finger to the hind legs.

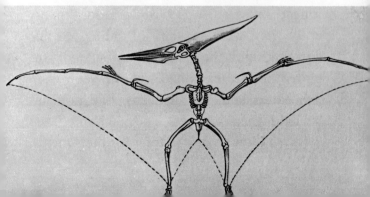

There is no evidence from the fossil records that they had the muscles necessary for prolonged flying such as birds can do. Apparently they were masters of riding the air currents, and they must have soared and glided hour after hour. Some of them were fish eaters and, like pelicans, had pouches to hold their catches. They skimmed the calm, shallow seas searching for their meals.

Many flying reptiles soared over shallow
seas 150 million years ago. Two were the
rudder-tailed Rhamphorhynchus
and big-headed Dimorphodon.

Flying reptiles did not survive the changes
in the earth's climate that came about some
60 million years ago. Like the equally odd
dinosaurs, they disappeared. Few modern
reptiles are capable of gliding flight.

Archaeopteryx, most ancient of the birds,
possessed many reptilian features. These
are seen clearly in the remarkable fossils found
in limestone quarries in Bavaria.

The First Feathers

DURING the same period in earth's history that reptiles developed their batlike wings, the first birds also appeared. The two most ancient birds known were identified from fossil remains discovered in limestone pits in Germany. One was named *Archaeopteryx,* meaning "ancient wing." The other was called *Archaeornis,* meaning "ancient bird."

These first birds were about the size of crows, and they looked very much like lizards with feathers. They had teeth and long tails, and there were claws on three free fingers. But they did have feathers! There were long flight feathers on their wings, and there were feathers over portions of their bodies. There was even a double row of feathers down each side of their tails.

From these primitive types came modern birds, the most successful of all flying animals. From the start, their wings had the sturdy support of the bones in their arms, and spread over them were Nature's newest contrivance—feathers—replacing the reptilian scales.

How Birds Fly

A BIRD is highly specialized for flight. Its bones are hollow, thus lightening the load that it must lift and keep in the air. A pelican's bony skeleton, for example, weighs less than a pound and a half, compared to the bird's total weight of about 25 pounds. But a bird's skeleton is also compact. Bones that are separate in other backboned animals are fused in the bird's skeleton. This reduces their bulk and at the same time adds to their strength. Many bones fit together in such a way as to form triangles, the strongest structural shape possible. The breastbone is drawn out into a keel to which the powerful flight muscles are attached. In strong fliers, these muscles may equal half the total weight of the bird.

Connected to the bird's lungs are numerous thin-walled cavities that are filled with air. These help to lessen the bird's weight and also serve as oxygen storage reservoirs to take care of the bird's great energy demands. Because of its constant activity, a bird burns fuel rapidly, maintaining a body temperature of 104 degrees or higher.

Over the bird's body is a covering of feathers. Those close to its body are soft and downy. They trap the air and make an insulating blanket which holds in body heat. Outside these there is a layer of smooth feathers, overlapping like the shingles on a roof. They seal in the air below and let the air outside slip over the bird's body with the least amount of friction.

The compactness of birds' skeletons and the simplicity and strength of their structure are shown here in the Australian wood kingfisher.

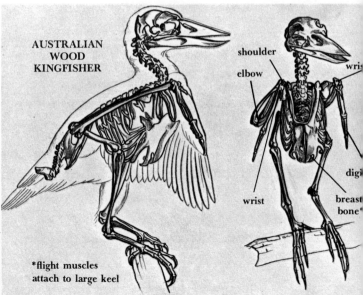

AUSTRALIAN
WOOD
KINGFISHER

shoulder

elbow

wris

wrist

dig

breast
bone*

*flight muscles
attach to large keel

The bird's body is also streamlined. All of its vital organs are pulled into a concentrated teardrop shape, with the most weight forward and beneath the wings where the lifting power is greatest.

The bird's flight feathers are attached to its wings. These feathers present a lightweight planing surface. But one of the marvels of bird flight is that groups of feathers can be moved independently. Air can be made to flow over them or through them or

Feathers insulate a bird's body, and numerous air spaces in the feathers add to buoyancy.

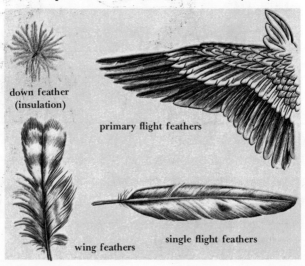

down feather
(insulation)

primary flight feathers

single flight feathers

wing feathers

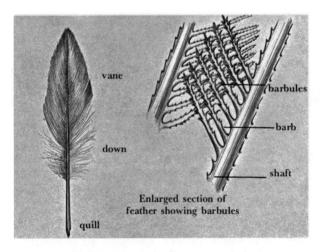

vane

down

quill

barbules

barb

shaft

Enlarged section of
feather showing barbules

**The feather is a hollow shaft with barbs extending
from its side fastened by barbules.**

to strike their surface at various angles. All
of this is controlled by the bird.

It is the remarkable structure of the bird's
feather that really makes flight possible. For
feathers are astonishingly strong, yet are
flexible and extremely light in weight. Each
arises from a hollow shaft, or quill, which
forms its center. From the sides of the shaft
extend a series of barbs, which altogether
form the flat surface, or vane, of the feather.
But each barb is further divided into smaller
units called barbules, and these, in turn, are

fastened together with tiny hooks, called barbicels. This adds up to some 20 or 30 million units per feather. Multiplied by the number of feathers over the bird's body it becomes a staggering figure well into the billions. These countless air spaces add to the bird's buoyancy. Yet each feather is laced together in a tight mesh capable of bending without breaking, withstanding all the rigorous stresses and strains of flight. It can be ruffled by the wind or pulled apart as the bird preens itself, yet with a single stroke of the bird's beak, it is rehooked to form the original flat, smooth surface.

Periodically a bird loses its feathers by moulting, but it loses them two at a time—one from each side. So even as old feathers are lost and new ones grow in, the bird retains its balance.

Only recently have we really learned how birds fly. Largely, this has been possible through the use of slow-motion photography so that the action of the wings could be studied. Now it is well understood that the movement of a bird's wings is far more complex than a simple flapping or "up and

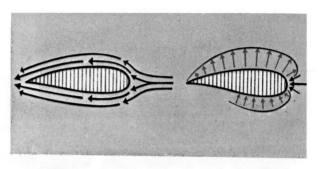

Air strikes the leading edge of the wing, traveling faster over the top. A greater density of air under the wing pushes up and gives the wing a lift.

down" motion. The wings are rotated, twisted, and turned in an amazing variety of ways, to achieve speed and direction.

The flapping movement "lifts" the bird into the air, just as the "up and down" stroke of the insect's wing lifts the insect. When the wings move down, the air below them is compressed. It is more dense than the air above the wings, so it presses against them and pushes the bird upward.

The bird's wing itself is streamlined. Its leading edge is thick and rounded, tapering to feather thinness at the rear. So when the bird moves forward or holds its wings outstretched into the wind, the air travels up

A barn swallow in flight

over the top and to the rear at a greater speed than it travels beneath the wing. The faster the bird flies or the stronger the wind blows, the more rapidly the air scoots over the top. A partial vacuum forms over the wing surface as the air stream strikes the front edge of the wing and bounces upward. This causes a greater pressure or density of air underneath the wing, which again pushes upward and gives the bird its "lift."

But a bird can also tilt its wings so that the angle at which the air strikes the leading edge of the wing is varied. This also alters the amount of air that slips over the upper surface and varies the amount of push from below. If the tilt becomes too great, the bird stalls—like an airplane. Then it must level off again to keep itself in the air.

The broad wings of the wood ibis allow it to soar easily on currents of wind.

The larger the surface area of the wing the more "lift" it has. This explains, at least in part, how the broadwinged turkey vulture literally floats through the sky, soaring and gliding hour after hour without moving its wings. Birds that do not have broad wings can also stay aloft without flapping their wings if they have sufficient speed. Once they are going fast, they can coast for a while, for the faster the air moves over their wings the greater the lift that is achieved. Hawks sometimes use this principle to ride the air currents, often seeming to do so for the sheer pleasure of it.

As a bird flaps its wings, the outer tips are rotated. They make the same sort of "figure 8" pattern that an insect's wings do in flight. The shape and size of the loops in the figure 8 are varied with the bird's speed and its direction of flight. So the bird's wings actually perform two functions at once. The sections close to its body remain almost level. They are the "lifters," like the wings of an airplane. The long primary feathers at its wing tips, however, supply the power for forward movement.

The Baltimore oriole (above) and the blue jay
(bottom) are shown in two flight positions in which
the wings are rotated. On the upward stroke,
the feathers of the wings are widely separated,
allowing air to pass through with least resistance.

The outer tips of a robin's wings begin to
rotate in a figure 8 pattern.

As the wing tips move downward, the
air passes over the front of the feathers
more rapidly than over the back. So the
bird is pushed forward by the increased air
pressure at the rear. Basically, this is the
same principle which "lifts" the bird into
the air, but the direction of the push is
changed from "up" to "forward."

And while these are the two basic forces which keep a bird in the air and drive it forward, there are almost as many variations in their use as there are kinds of birds.

First, of course, the bird must get off the ground. Most birds jump into the air, at the same time flapping their wings rapidly to get air speed. They spend many times more energy in becoming airborne than they do at any other stage of flying. Some kinds of ducks do this rapidly. Pelicans, in

Like most flying or gliding animals, perching birds spring into the air to fly.

Some ducks spring into the air to take off; others skitter over the sea to get into the air.

contrast, have a slow take-off, sometime skimming the surface for long distances before they can rise. Other water birds flap their wings and at the same time run across the surface to get enough speed to get into the air.

Quails, grouse, woodcocks, and similar birds have short wings. They fly fast but not far. Their wings are too short to give them much "lift," and so they depend greatly on their speed. Their take-off is rapid and noisy, the wind whistling through the spread, stiff feathers of their wing tips. In contrast, vultures often have to wait until the morning sun has begun to create thermal currents of air before they can leave their roost. They can fly by flapping their wings, but this is hard work for them. They depend on the winds and the drafts of air. For speed and distance, a bird's wings are long and narrow, like a swallow's or a hawk's.

But even an albatross, one of the best long-distance fliers, cannot stay in the air

Hawks have medium-length, pointed wings for fast, powerful flight to capture prey.

Long, narrow wings of an albatross make it the best of the sea-soaring birds.

forever. Eventually a bird must land, and this, too, takes some degree of skill. The bird glides toward the spot where it intends to land, and at the appropriate moment, it spreads its tail and lifts its body and its wings. These strike the air flatly, thus stalling the bird's flight. At the same time the bird stretches out its feet to touch its perch.

Occasionally a bird does misjudge its distances and speed and may circle several times before landing. Ducks often literally plummet into the water.

Birds do make mistakes in flying, but all in all, their mastery of the air is amazing. Watch a cloud of chimney swifts wheeling and turning, almost brushing wing tips, as they flutter over their sooty roost and drop in one by one. Follow a swirling flock of starlings on the way to their roost, and see how swiftly they fly and how quickly they follow each other's turns.

Before landing, a mallard spreads its tail and elevates its body to brake forward motion.

Hummingbirds are the most versatile fliers.
They can fly forward, backward, sideways,
up, or down—and can also hover
to get the nectar from a flower.

Most versatile of all are the humming-birds. There are some 600 species of these agile aerialists, most of them found only in the tropics. They have extremely short forearms—the section of the wing which gives other birds their soaring and gliding power. But the hand section of their wings is highly developed and maneuverable. Thus, their flight is accomplished mostly in the manner of a helicopter—with propellers only. And, like the helicopter they can move forward, sideways, backwards, up, or down—all at great speed.

Their wings hum loudly, vibrating as rapidly as 200 times per second and averaging 50. In contrast, pelicans, storks, and other large-winged, slow-flying birds may flap their wings only about two times per second. Most of the songbirds flap their wings about 10 or 12 times per second.

Even more astonishing for such small creatures, hummingbirds are also long-distance fliers. Every autumn some species leave the mainland of the United States and fly across the Gulf of Mexico, a distance of more than 500 miles nonstop. In the spring they return. At 50 miles an hour, like jeweled bullets, they wing their way over the water. Other birds can fly faster, and many can fly farther. But in proportion to size, none are more remarkable than the tiny hummingbirds.

Fastest of the birds are the duckhawks. They are believed to attain speeds of more

The figures below are maximum flight speeds rather than normal flying speeds of these birds.

BLUE JAY   20 MPH

HERRING GULL   35 MPH

GREAT HORNED OWL   40 MPH

STARLING   50 MPH

CANADA GOOSE   70 MPH

HUMMINGBIRD   70 MPH

GOLDEN EAGLE   80 MPH

PEREGRINE HAWK   100 MPH

The **long distance flying** record is held by
the arctic tern, which flies 24,000 miles.

than 180 miles per hour in dives. Many
ducks and geese can fly at 50 or 60 miles
per hour, as can swifts, plovers, crows, and
hawks. Songbirds, although they appear to
be going faster, seldom exceed 20 miles per
hour.

The record for distance flying is held by
the arctic tern which journeys 24,000 miles,
from the Arctic to the Antarctic and back
again each year. Golden plovers fly nonstop

from Labrador to South America, 2,400 miles across the Atlantic Ocean. On their return, they cross the Gulf of Mexico.

Canada geese fly in close formation, changing direction swiftly without hitting each other.

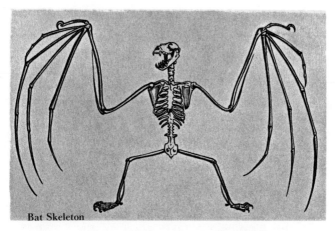

Bat Skeleton

A bat's membranous wings are strengthened by
being spread over the bones of four fingers.

Furry Fliers

INSECTS, birds, and bats are the only living
animals capable of true flight: that is, able
to control both their direction and their
speed. Of the three, bats are in many ways
the most unusual.

Like the extinct flying reptiles, bats have
wings consisting of thin membranes of skin
stretched between their legs and their bodies.
Even their hind legs are attached to this
membrane, and in many species the membrane is continued between their hind legs

and their tails, adding to the "lift" surface.

But the membranous wings of the bat are much stronger than were the similar wings of flying reptiles. Four of the bat's fingers, rather than only one, are lengthened to form the framework over which the wing membranes are tightly stretched.

Bats fly by flapping their wings. Attached to a ridge on their breastbones are strong flight muscles. Narrow-winged bats that live in the tropics are fast, graceful fliers. They

As bats fly, they emit high-frequency squeaks that echo from objects in their path.

are easily mistaken for swifts. But most bats fly floppily, much like butterflies. They do not appear to be as sure of themselves in the air as birds are. Yet bats fly "blind" —on instruments, so to speak. They can weave their way through a maze of thin wires hung in their path without even brushing them lightly. This strange navigation system works on a radar principle. It is used by only one species of bird: the guacharo, or oilbird, which is also nocturnal and lives in caves in northern South America.

As the bat flies, it emits shrill, high-frequency noises. Some of these sounds can be heard by the human ear, but most are supersonic. Their frequency ranges from 30 to 70 kilocycles. Humans can hear only about 20 kilocycles.

Oddly, the bat itself does not hear these sounds when they are first emitted, for as each sound is given off, a special set of muscles close the bat's ears. As the bat flies, it may emit as many as 30 of these sounds every second. When it comes closer to some object, it may increase the frequency of the noises to about 60 per second.

Enlarged ears on bats' faces help in picking up
high-frequency echolocation signals.

When one of these high-frequency pulses
strikes a solid object nearby, it bounces back.
The bat hears the echo, for its ears are closed
only when it gives off the sounds. Some
bats have special, "leafy" folds of skin over
their faces to help their large and sensitive
ears detect these echoes.

The supersonic sounds given off by the
bat do not travel far. Twenty feet is about
maximum. They bounce back only about
15 feet. But this gives the bat time enough
to swerve quickly and avoid any object in
its path. The short range of transmission pre-
vents one bat from interfering with the navi-
gational system of another or from getting
delayed echoes as a result of its own trans-
missions. Interestingly, bats turn off this

supersonic system when they enter caves, hollow trees, or other places to roost. It is also put out of operation when they have a mouthful of food. At these times the bats may hit objects, or they can be caught in nets which they would ordinarily avoid.

Most unbelievable (and still unexplained) is the ability of a bat to distinguish between an object to avoid and something to eat. For a bat can turn and twist its way through the branches of a tree, then swiftly swoop over a particular leaf and pluck an insect from it. All of this takes place in darkness, of course, and the bat's eyes are good for

A bat, loose in a darkened room, can fly through a maze of wires without touching them.

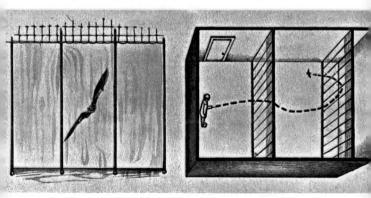

little more than telling day from night. Perhaps the bat can detect heat, almost imperceptible amounts, given off by the insect's body.

The bat's tail is often used when it makes its landings, for then the membranous pocket between its tail and its hind legs fills with air and acts like a brake. At the same time the bat lifts its wings to stall its forward motion so that it flutters to a gentle landing.

Some bats can take off directly from the ground, but it is easier for them to drop from some elevation, combining gliding and flapping flight to get their air speed. Bats perch by hanging with their heads down. This makes launching easy. All they do is spread their wings as they let go. Some kinds flap their wings while they are still holding onto the perch, and they do not let go until their bodies have been lifted almost to a horizontal position.

"Flying foxes," fruit bats found in Africa, Asia, and Australia, are the largest of the bats. A species found in Java has a wingspread of five feet. These giants are skilled at flying and may travel long distances.

A red bat and its young perch by hanging
upside down from a rafter.

There are other bats about the size of hummingbirds that are capable of the same type of fast or hovering flight. It is believed that some species can travel as rapidly as 35 miles per hour. Others make nonstop flights of 500 miles or more.

The brown bat is found throughout
most of North America.

Gliding Animals

SOME "winged" animals use their wings only for gliding. This is the first step toward true flight. Many of these gliders can travel long distances if they have the help of the wind or have launched themselves from high places. Most of them remain airborne for only a hundred yards or so at the maximum, however.

Flights of a quarter of a mile have been reported for flying fish. These unusual creatures have enlarged fins which stick out at the sides of their bodies like wings. Generally, the flying fish takes to the air when it is being chased by some hungry larger fish, such as a dolphin, but there are times, apparently, when the flying fish "flies" strictly for the pleasure of being in the air.

To become airborne, it literally swims out of the water. Swimming as rapidly as it can just beneath the surface, it turns up suddenly and bursts from the water, driving itself into the air with powerful thrusts of its tail. Young flying fish continue to vibrate their fin wings after they are in the air. They seem to be trying to flap them to continue

**Flying fish spread their wing-like pectoral fins
and glide hundreds of yards over the sea.**

flying. The movement is rapid, and the wings
make a rattling sound, due to the wind
rather than to special muscular effort. In
large flying fish, the wings seldom move.

Flying fish do their best gliding when
there is a good wind blowing. Headed into
the wind they can stay in the air for glides
that carry them hundreds of yards. At times,
over a trough in the sea, they may be five
or six feet above the water. They can turn
and bank to change directions, and when

they come close to the surface, they may drop their tails into the water and vibrate them rapidly to maintain their flight speed.

True flying fishes are natives of tropical seas. There they are abundant, both in numbers and kinds. Some species are most active at night, frequently landing on the decks of ships. Unlike bats and guacharos, they have no mechanism for detecting objects in their paths.

In Africa and South America, there are fresh-water fishes capable of similar short, gliding flights, and the flying gurnard, a member of the sea robin family, can also glide. Even giant rays will occasionally leap clear of the water and sail through the air. Flapping their broad winglike pectoral fins, which are really useful to them only underwater, they look like huge bats. Their brief journeys into space always end in belly-smacking splats as they hit the surface of the water again.

None of the amphibians—toads, frogs, or salamanders—have developed wings, but a tree frog that lives in Asia can parachute to the ground or from tree to tree. Between

One Asiatic frog has long webbed toes.
These serve as parachutes when the frog
jumps from high places.

its widespread toes there are enormous folds
of skin, and when the frog jumps, these
webs catch the air so that the frog half
glides and half parachutes through space.

No present-day reptiles are as well
equipped for gliding as their ancestors were,
but some can glide short distances. Several
kinds of gliding snakes are found in Asia.
They prepare for their glides by first deflat-
ing their lungs, thus flattening their bodies.
Then they lift their extra-long ribs, pulling

the skin tightly over them. When they launch themselves from a tree, they appear to be not much thicker than blades of grass. And with a leaflike, wavering flutter, they drift toward the ground or into nearby foliage in a slanting glide.

The "flying dragon," a lizard that lives in the same area, is also a glider. It has

Tree-dwelling snakes of southern Asia flatten their bodies and glide from tree to tree.

**The flying dragon is a gliding lizard
that lives in southeastern Asia.**

loose folds of skin along the sides of its
body, and its ribs are extraordinarily long.
When its ribs are raised, the loose skin
stretches over them to make gliding surfaces
from leg to leg. The lizard can easily glide
several hundred feet, from tree to tree without ever touching the ground.

Among mammals, the best known gliders
are the so-called "flying" squirrels, found
in the woodlands of the United States and
Canada. Their flight membranes are
stretched between their front and hind
legs. Their tails are used as rudders when
the little animals are in gliding flight.

Flying squirrels launch themselves from high up in a tree, and they can glide through the forest a hundred yards or more. Generally their glides are short, the distance depending on the height from which they start their glide. Flying squirrels turn sharply, descend steeply—then level off. They can make all sorts of maneuvers short of actual flight. In landing, they lift their tails and their bodies sharply, settling as softly as autumn leaves.

There are also flying squirrels in northern Europe and in Africa. There, too, the little animals are normally active only at night, and few people get to see them in action.

Flying squirrels have furry flight membranes of skin between front and hind legs.

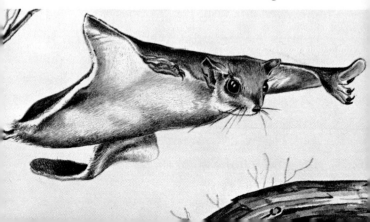

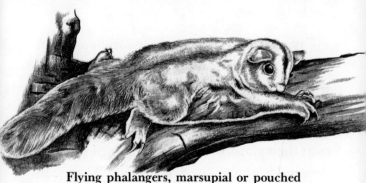

Flying phalangers, marsupial or pouched
mammals of Australia, are nocturnal gliders.

During the day they stay hidden in hollow
trees, but sometimes they are disturbed from
these lodging places. Then the forest may
become suddenly alive with gliding creatures as a hundred or more take to the air.

In Australia, there are flying phalangers.
These are "pouched" animals, like kanga-
roos and opossums, and they range in size
from some no larger than mice to others
that are bigger than cats. Their long tails
are used as grasping organs, and with the
same sort of membrane as the flying squir-
rel's, these animals may glide long distances.

Finally, in southern Asia there are the
so-called "flying lemurs," or colugos. Closely
related to bats, they look more like flying
squirrels. Their flight membranes extend

onto their necks and are also stretched between their hind legs and their tails. There
are even webs between the fingers of their
hands. Flying lemurs are excellent gliders.
Females can even carry their young as they
glide from tree to tree.

**Flying lemurs, or colugos, are more closely
related to bats than to lemurs.**

On the Wind

SOME kinds of animals (and plants, too) travel long distances on the wind. Many are especially designed for this type of air travel. In nature's scheme, it is a convenient way of distributing them throughout the world. Wind travelers have no control over their speed or direction, coming to rest wherever the wind deposits them.

**Powerful winds may pick up small animals and
"rain" them to the ground miles away.**

Tiny microscopic plants and animals are
frequent air travelers. Some ride about on
particles of dust. Others are immersed in
droplets of water, and still others secrete
heavy outer coverings which prevent them
from drying out during journeys that may
last for months or even years. Bacteria are

especially abundant in the air over the earth. They may drift from continent to continent with the wind. Others may be suspended in the air, spinning and whirling their way through space, involuntarily in orbit about the earth.

Even large animals are often picked up by the wind. All sorts of spiders, mites, snails—animals that never had intentions of going into the air—may suddenly find themselves snatched up by the wind and set down (or dropped) in some unfamiliar land. In strong winds, such as tornadoes or hurricanes, even animals capable of flight are buffeted about. This explains how birds from the United States appear in England and how birds of the tropics find themselves as far up the east coast of North America as Maine. Powerful updrafts may suck such heavier-than-air creatures as fish, shrimp, mice, rats, or similar animals into the sky and shower them down again miles away.

Insects in particular are often carried by the wind. In some cases this is part of nature's way of distributing them. Winged ants and termites, for example, are poor fliers, but with the aid of the wind they soon establish colonies well separated from each other.

The spring air is frequently filled with insects that have just hatched and are seeking their places in the world. Even immature insects sometimes fly with the wind. Young gypsy moth caterpillars, for example, are thickly covered with hollow hairs. These make the little caterpillars so buoyant that they are easily dislodged from their perches and moved by the wind. They have been known to travel as far as five miles a day in this manner.

Young gypsy moth caterpillars are easily carried by the wind because of their buoyancy.

**On strands of silk, "ballooning" spiders
ride the wind for hundreds of miles.**

Spiders are the animal kingdom's master
balloonists. In the fall of the year, young
balloon spiders climb to the tops of plants,
rocks, or other elevations and prepare to
launch themselves into the wind. First they
let out a single strand of silk which is carried into the sky by the wind. This is followed by another and still another until

the spider's abdomen is lifted off its lodging. Thread by thread the spider hoists itself into the air until at last it sails away. Ballooning spiders have been found floating on air currents nearly three miles above the surface of the earth and hundreds of miles out at sea. Many that inhabit offshore islands got there by ballooning their way across the water.

Even the plant kingdom has its airborne travelers. Ripened seeds of maples, elms, and ash break away from the parent trees

Paired seeds of maples whirl in the wind
like blades of a helicopter.

when the wind blows. Whirling like propellers on the loose, they may travel hundreds of yards before settling back to earth.
The seeds of the dandelion, milkweed, and
similar plants are even better designed for
long distance air travel. Lighter than feathers, they can ride the lightest breeze.

The wind is unquestionably one of the
most important distributors of plants and
animals.

**Dandelion seeds are attached to feathery tufts
that drift with the slightest wind.**

INDEX

*illustration only